Tried and True
Classroom Games and Greetings

ORIGINS **DEVELOPMENTAL DESIGNS**®

Grades 4–9

ISBN 978-0-938541-00-4
Library of Congress Control Number 2010936886

Edited by Linda Crawford
Cover and book design and illustrations by Heidi Neilson
Cover photograph by Jennifer Bush

All net proceeds from the sale of *Tried and True Classroom Games and Greetings: Grades 4–9* support the work of The Origins Program, a nonprofit educational organization whose mission is to promote an equitable and humane multicultural society through quality education for all.

The Origins Program
3805 Grand Avenue South
Minneapolis, Minnesota 55409 USA
800-543-8715
www.developmentaldesigns.org

17 16 15 14   6 5 4 3

This book supports the *Developmental Designs* approach to integrating social-emotional and academic learning in the middle grades. The approach uses best practices for building social skills, positive relationships, and high engagement to create optimal conditions for learning. See pages 70–71 to learn more about the approach and other supporting resources from The Origins Program.

⚭ DEVELOPMENTAL DESIGNS®

Helping Adolescents Succeed in School

This book was developed through the work of The Origins Program, a nonprofit educational organization and creator of the *Developmental Designs*™ approach. The approach consists of highly practical strategies designed to integrate social and academic learning for adolescents, increase motivation and self-management, and strengthen connections to school.

Developmental Designs Teaching Practices

Advisory: Circle of Power and Respect and Advisory Plus

Empowering Language

Goal Setting

Social Contract

Modeling and Practicing

The Loop

Power of Play

Pathways to Self-control

Problem-solving Strategies

Practices for Motivating Instruction

Learn More about the *Developmental Designs* Approach

Professional Development Opportunities

- Six- to thirty-hour learning experiences for middle-level educators
- Consultant-guided learning to support implementation
- School-wide consultation to provide support for sustainability

Publications and Resources for Middle-Level Educators

- Other publications supporting the *Developmental Designs* approach:
  The Advisory Book: Building a Community of Learners Grades 5-9
  The Advisory Book Study Guide (for professional development with colleagues)
  Classroom Discipline: Guiding Adolescents to Responsible Independence
  Classroom Discipline Study Guide (for professional development with colleagues)
  The Circle of Power and Respect Advisory Meeting DVD
  Modeling and Practicing Classroom Routines DVD
  Face to Face Advisories
  Developmental Designs Self-Coaching Guide
- Free weekly blogs to support beginning and experienced *Developmental Designs* practitioners
- Online resources that include video clips and hundreds of articles and activities to support implementation

Order at www.developmentaldesigns.org or call (800) 543-8715 M-F: 9-5, CT

WORKSHOPS • CONSULTING • BOOKS & RESOURCES

Introduction

Tried and True Classroom Games and Greetings is comprised of the games, greetings, shares, and acknowledgments that experienced teachers of adolescents have found to be community-building favorites. These are the ones they use over and over because they are no-fail fun-providers and friendship-builders, even on gray Monday mornings or when standardized tests are looming.

Games, greetings, shares, and acknowledgments contents:

- 30 games. Some are active, some quiet. Many help build trust, and all help meet young people's need to have fun.

- 20 greetings. Fun greetings in a basic greeting structure, and other greetings that involve intriguing patterns and variations. All build community, and all allow participants to show that everyone belongs.

- 5 shares. These get-to-know-you activities are fun ways to practice conversational skills, interviewing, or speaking to a group. All meet participants' needs for relationship and feelings of competence.

- 12 acknowledgments. Nine fun ways to cheer for completing a project, a school week, a test, or for any accomplishment; and three that call on participants to affirm one another personally and powerfully. All are interactive and engaging, and all foster mutual appreciation.

- 5 blank pages to get you started adding your own class favorites

The Power of Relationship

Games infuse the community with the positive power of play. Greeting each other by name shows that we all belong. Sharing is the way people get acquainted on a personal level and discover commonalities. Acknowledgments reinforce individuals and the group for persevering or for trying something new. These social activities glue the group together in a community committed to shared success.

A Way to Help Young People Step Up and Lead

The instructions on these pages are easy to follow. They are designed to empower leaders of community-building activities with one successful experience after another. Try variations of your own. Open up the clasp and use the blank pages provided at the back of the book to add more games, greetings, sharing formats, and acknowledgments that your class enjoys.

Games Introduction

Play is one of the most powerful tools teachers have to facilitate the internalization of learning. Students experience games on physical, emotional, social, and intellectual levels simultaneously. Everyone has to learn the rules, interact with others in a controlled manner, and experience winning, losing, and encouraging each other. Harder, more challenging games can stretch the players toward responsible independence.

Game levels:

Community Level 1, Acquainted: Help members of newly formed groups get to know one another and practice respectful play; low-risk questions and activities characterize these games

Community Level 2, Familiar: Good for groups who have learned a bit about one another and have played together successfully; more physical and mental challenge and silliness raise the social risk in these games; may include elimination

Community Level 3, Comfortable: The laughter, movement, and mental challenge in these games invite groups who have played together repeatedly with success to enjoy and deepen their community bonds

Educators use their judgment as to where on the continuum their groups fall at any particular time. For example, one class may be ready for "familiar" games at the end of Week Two, while another class may need to wait much longer.

List of Games

Games Contents

* Minimal transition or movement and no circle required

GAMES INTRODUCTION

Arm Hockey

Material: Soft ball, 6" to 10" in diameter

Players stand in a circle facing the center, each player's legs a little wider than shoulder width apart and neighbors' feet touching. Players use their non-dominant arm/hand—the one they don't normally use to write—to try to hit the ball between another player's legs (goal) and to guard against the ball going through their goal. The ball must be hit only with the palm of the hand and must be kept on the floor.

✱ Model and practice hitting the ball safely with an open palm.

Variations

- Teams may be formed into two half circles or two straight lines, and a game played up to a predetermined score.

- Players may be declared out if they allow a goal to be scored through their legs. In this case, they are allowed back into the game when another player is scored upon. Discuss with players beforehand the skill of losing gracefully.

- Game may be played sitting in chairs with the spaces between the chair legs as the goals, feet placed outside of the chair legs.

- Game can be played either with one hand (non-dominant) or two (only the defenders may use two hands; players attempting to score still must use only their non-dominant hands).

Also known as Elephant Soccer, Circle Hockey

ARM HOCKEY
game

Aunt Minerva

The person who begins the activity decides on a category such as "flat things" but does not tell anyone else. Instead, she gives several examples to demonstrate the category by telling things that Aunt Minerva likes and does not like. For example, if the category is flat things she might say:

Aunt Minerva likes tables but does not like balls. Aunt Minerva likes slate but does not like oranges. Aunt Minerva likes ice rinks but does not like hills.

The other players try to figure out the category. When they think they know the category, they give an example of something Aunt Minerva likes and an example of something she doesn't like. The person who began the activity says whether the guesser is right or not. The leader gives more examples and listens to others' guesses until many players have shown they know the category by saying something Aunt Minerva likes and something she doesn't like. For maximum engagement, end one round and begin another before there are only a handful of players still wondering.

★Model and practice selecting and discovering simple, irrefutable, non-relative categories, such as the example above of flat things. Discuss why categories such as "hot" are relative and not appropriate to this game. Consider using these non-relative categories: sharp, round, square, flat, fluid, frozen, solid, container, bound, flying, swimming, floating, nouns, and verbs.

Variation

- **Green Door:** As in Aunt Minerva, the game leader gives an example that fits the category, but doesn't name the category. The leader says, *I shall bring a* (example) *through the green door.* Guessers deduce the category by requesting to bring a variety of things through the door. The items can be objects, numbers, or ideas. Players ask, *May I bring a _____ through the green door?* The leader replies *Yes* or *No*. Play ends when several people have made correct guesses, and a player names the topic, or when time is up.

Green Door example

Topic: Adjectives, followed by the nouns they modify

Leader:	*I shall bring a red brick through the green door.*
Player 1:	*May I bring a football through the green door?* (thinking the topic is nouns)
Leader:	*No, you may not.*
Player 2:	*May I bring a red car through the green door?*
Leader:	*Yes, you may.*

After five or six correct guesses from other players, continue:

Leader:	*What is my category?*
Player 7:	*Your category is adjectives, followed by the nouns they modify.*

Players stand in a circle. It tells a player to make one of three poses: Elvis, Elephant or Surfer Dude. Each pose requires three people. The person called on to do the pose is the middle person, and the two players sitting on either side must help.

- For Elvis, the middle person poses as if playing a guitar; the two on either side are the fans, waving their hands overhead.
- For the Surfer Dude, the middle person stands and moves as if riding a surfboard; the two on either side are the water, with hands waving side to side at waist height.
- For the Elephant, the middle person joins her two hands together with arms extended to make the trunk; the two on either side put their arms into "C" shapes to make large ears on either side of the elephant's "head."

Depending on the pose selected, the person who is It tries to say *Elephant/Elvis/Surfer Dude, Bippity Bop Bop Bop*, before the three people create the pose. The middle person in the group that doesn't make their pose in time becomes It. If all three succeed, It moves around the circle and calls on another player to make Elvis, Elephant or Surfer Dude.

✴Model and practice the three actions without timing, then with timing. Teach this game after a strong community is established, probably later in the year.

Variation

Players can invent additional poses for groups of three or five people. Another popular pose is Cockroach, where one person assumes the form of a bug on its back, arms, and legs wiggling in the air, and the other two at her side pretend to spray insecticide. Model and practice each new pose before it is incorporated into play. The fun and challenge increase as the number of possible poses increases.

Material: Something to pass behind backs, such as a small stuffed animal (the "weasel")

Players stand shoulder-to-shoulder in a circle facing center. One player is It and stands in the middle of the circle. The players chant rhythmically: *Bob the weasel, keep him going, keep him going,* as they bob up and down. They pass the weasel behind their backs, trying to hide the object from It. When It spots the weasel, he points to the person holding it and then trades places with the person who was holding the weasel when spotted.

★ Model and practice keeping the weasel moving at all times and chanting in a friendly manner.

Variations

- Use a stick or stone as the passing piece with the chant:
  Stick, stick (or stone, stone) how you wander
  From one hand into the other
  Is it fair?
  Is it fair?
  To keep poor _____ (It's name) standing there!

- Bitty Bitty version: Pass a ring with the chant:
  Bitty, Bitty, hold on!
  Lost my gold ring!
  Go down to Kingston,
  Come back again.

- When It is not looking, a player with the weasel holds it up for others to see. Players who saw the weasel chant *We saw the weasel. We saw the weasel.*

The leader and players repeat the following chant and make dance movements or pantomime characters.

Leader: *Let me see your boogalu!*
Group: *What's that you say?*
Leader: *I said, let me see your boogalu!*
Group: *What's that you say?*
Leader: *I say Oo oo oo oo oo oo oo!* (boogalu action in rhythm)
Group: *I say Oo oo oo oo oo oo oo!* (repeat action in rhythm)

Repeat the chant with a new leader, or keep the same leader, replacing "boogalu" with another subject.
For example: *Let me see your Frankenstein* (or *your beauty queen; your rock star; your happy baby; your angry tiger*, etc.)

The leader role can move around the circle (allowing reluctant players to pass), or can move to whoever volunteers. Each new leader invents his own boogalu action.

★Model and practice a few rounds of the game and spark some ideas. Players may choose from a category or take time to create a character and an action. This is a fun game with lots of laughter!

This game expands on the game of Rock, Paper, Scissors. Players become the following characters by doing the character's actions:

Coconut (walking on knees or squatting with bent knees)
Palm Tree (swaying arms overhead)
Volcano (jumping using arms as lava)
King or Queen Most-Exalted (doing a royal wave)

All players start as Coconuts (walking on knees or squatting with bent knees). Each finds another Coconut and the two play Rock, Paper, Scissors. Whoever wins evolves up to become a Palm Tree (standing and swaying arms overhead); whoever loses remains a Coconut. After each game, players find other players of their own kind and play Rock, Paper, Scissors again. Winners evolve up (winning Palm Trees become Volcanoes; winning Volcanoes become King or Queen Most-Exalted) and the losers evolve down (Kings and Queens become Volcanoes, Volcanoes become Palm Trees, etc.). Players try to move up to King or Queen Most-Exalted, but the game is continuous.

✱Model and practice the roles and, with younger players, review Rock, Paper, Scissors. Model safe movement within whatever space is defined for the game. Set a time limit.

One player will be the seeker, and stands outside the circle in a location where she cannot see the group. The group silently chooses a leader, who does a movement, such as tapping his toe, which the other players copy. The leader changes the movement regularly, and the other players copy the leader's new movement. The object is for the seeker to identify the leader.

When the group has its leader, the seeker returns and stands in the middle of the circle. She watches the movements and tries to guess who the leader is. The seeker has three chances to identify the leader. After the leader has been identified or the player in the middle has had three guesses, another seeker and secret leader are chosen to start another round.

✱Model and practice strategies to help the seeker discover the leader, or to help the leader avoid being discovered. If it is too hard for younger players to guess while standing inside the circle, allow the seeker to stand outside of the circle to guess.

Variations

- Choose more than one seeker at a time and allow them to confer before guessing.
- Limit the number of guesses.
- Choose two leaders, who take turns starting new movements.
- Use movements that make no sound (makes it harder!).

Curtain Call

Materials: Blanket, sheet, or curtain; two chairs

Two players hold up a blanket or sheet (the curtain). Place an empty chair close to each side of the curtain. Players form two groups, one group on each side of the curtain. One player from each group takes a seat in the chair provided. The leader signals to drop the curtain, and the two players who are seated race to name the other player then revealed and facing them. The one named first joins the group on the other side of the curtain. The curtain is raised again, a new person occupies each chair, and the game is repeated, and so on. The team with more players wins when time runs out.

★ Model and practice rotating the players holding the curtain every few rounds or with every round of naming. The leader gives as many people as possible a turn at the chairs.

Variations

- The game is over when all players are on one side of the curtain.
- Players try to identify each other by voices only.

Deer Watcher

Material: Flashlight for one variation

Group is arranged in a circle of watchers, and one person, the deer, is in the center. The watchers take positions that they can hold perfectly still. The deer's job is to watch for any movement of a watcher and snort (make a sound with nose/mouth that sounds like a deer snorting) in the direction of a person who makes a movement. Watchers can move when they think they are out of the deer's view, but when caught moving, they are out. If a watcher smiles or laughs when the deer snorts at someone else, he is out. (Blinking is allowed.) The last watcher standing wins the game, and can become the next deer, if you play another round.

✶ Model and practice possible frozen-walking and frozen-looking gestures for watcher poses.

Variations

- Watchers try to sneak up and lightly touch the deer without being detected. If successful at touching the deer, the watcher gets a turn at being the deer, and a new round starts.

- **Museum:** Players assume the posture of a sculpture (if the museum is said to be an art museum) or an animal (if it's a natural history museum), etc. The museum guard stands in the center of the circle, but when the guard is not looking, the posers come to life. If the guard catches one moving, she shines her flashlight on it and the mover is out. The last sculpture or animal standing becomes the guard in the next round.

Players form circles of four or so, their hands behind their backs. A leader gives the signal to start each round of play. On the leader's signal, each person puts one hand forward, one to five fingers extended. Each group's goal is to flash a total of 11 fingers among the players in their group. Collaborative strategizing is prohibited—players have to "intuit" what others might do.

✶ Model and practice how to flash fingers on the signal. Choose a clear signal to start play.

Variations

- When a group totals 11, they cheer, and then each player in that group joins another group. If two groups total 11 in one round, all groups reconfigure, with no players in the same group twice.

- Change the total number to be achieved.

Players are evenly distributed among four corners of a room; the corners are named North, South, East, and West. A caller in the center closes his eyes and says, *Corners.* While his eyes are closed, the players silently change corners at random. The caller then names a corner by saying *North, South, East,* or *West.* Players who are standing in the corner that is called are out. If anyone fails to reach a corner before the caller calls out, she is also out. The game continues until the four corners are empty. Begin another round with a new caller.

✷Model and practice safe movement between corners. Specify a minimum time the caller must wait before calling a corner. Designate where players go when they are out. Prepare players ahead of time to exercise good sportsmanship if they are called out.

Variations

- **Advisers:** Any players who are called out can become "advisers" to the caller. They huddle together in the middle and advise the caller what corner to call next.

- **Four Corner Thinking**: Corners or areas of the room are labeled with signs: Agree, Somewhat Agree, Somewhat Disagree, Disagree. The leader makes statements about a chosen topic. After each statement, players move to the corner that describes their response. Before making the next statement, the leader can ask players to explain why they chose their corner and share more about the opinion.

Four Corner Thinking examples

Topic: Energy conservation
Hybrid cars are the best way to save energy.
We save energy in this school.
I save energy in my home.
I would give up some of my personal comfort to save energy.

Topic: Wildlife management
We should try to manage wildlife.
Hunters should have more say about wildlife management.
Deer should be hunted year-round.

Gotcha!

Participants stand in a circle with left arms bent, hands raised to shoulder height, and flat palms facing up. They point the pointer finger of their right hands down into the middle of the palm of the person to the right. When the leader says *Gotcha!* participants try to grab the finger in their left palm and at the same time escape being grabbed on the right.

✱ Model and practice the positions of both right and left hands with another player. Demonstrate how to gently grab a finger.

Variations

- Switch sides so that everyone's right palm is up and left pointer fingers are pointing down.

- Do an upside-down Gotcha with palms facing down and pointer fingers facing up.

- Do a crossover Gotcha. Set it up the same way as the basic Gotcha with the left palm up and the right pointer finger pointing down into the palm of the person to the right. When the leader says, *Gotcha!,* each person's right hand crosses over in front of his body and tries to capture the pointer finger of the person to his left.

Group Juggle

Materials: Three to six small, soft balls or beanbags

Players stand in a circle. A player is selected to begin and is given a ball or beanbag. She says someone's name and, when she and the person she called make eye contact, she tosses the ball or beanbag to that person, who says another person's name and tosses it to that person, and so on, until each player has handled the ball once. The last player to receive the ball tosses it to the player who started. She may stop or keep the ball in play by tossing it to the same person she picked the first time, and the tossing continues in the same pattern. Nobody may handle the ball a second time until everyone has handled it once.

✱Model and practice getting a receiver's attention before throwing, and gently throwing underhand.

Variations

- When the group has mastered using one ball, have the starter toss more balls into play, always in the same pattern, until it becomes a group juggle with a number of balls in the air at once.

- Track the group's best time for one full round. Brainstorm and try ways to improve the group's time.

- **Toss the Name**: Players stand in a circle. Begin by having each player say his/her name. Next, the leader holds a ball and repeats his own name, *I am Steve*, then names a player and tosses the ball to her, *and this is Kris.* Kris catches the ball and says, *That is Steve, I am Kris, and this is Amanda*, and then tosses the ball to Amanda. After the leader's first toss, each player will say two names besides her own. The game continues until all have been called. To increase the challenge, add additional balls to juggle and use time-keeping.

- **Cumulative Toss the Name**: Adapt the Toss the Name variation by challenging players to name *all* of the players who came before them. For example, after three players have thrown the ball and have been named, the forth person says, *Those are Ralph, Mercedes, Calvin, Jose, Jessica, Tyril, I am Bonnie, and this is Grace.*

- See Beanbag Toss Greeting on page 51 for a greeting version of this game.

Material: Coin

Everybody stands in a circle. Each player signals a choice by holding one hand on his head (heads) or hip (tails). This pose is maintained while a coin is flipped. If it lands heads, all those who chose tails must sit down; if it lands tails, everyone who chose heads sits down. The game continues until one player remains; it is usually played with several rounds.

✴Model and practice moving rather quickly from round to round, so those who are sitting down are not idle for an extended time.

Variations

- Ask players to predict how many rounds it will take to reach one player standing.
- Ask players to think of strategies to shorten the number of rounds.
- Discuss probability.

A player is selected to exit the room. The group chooses an adverb that has the -ly suffix. The player returns. She then tries to figure out the secret adverb by requesting that individual players pantomime doing something "in the manner of the adverb." For example, *Jose, please wash dishes in the manner of the adverb.* Or, *Neela, please eat breakfast in the manner of the adverb.* Based on the pantomime, she guesses the secret adverb. If she doesn't get it, additional pantomimes may be given.

Decide in advance how many requests in the manner of the adverb the guessing player may make and how many guesses she gets after each pantomime.

★ Model and practice how to act out a task in the manner of an adverb.

Players are seated in a circle. One player is in the middle of the circle, and her chair is removed. Her objective is to get a seat. She approaches a seated player and asks, *Is this seat taken?* If the answer is *no*, the two exchange places, and the player who gave up her seat begins another round. If the answer is *yes*, she must ask another. As the player in the middle is asking various players for a seat, others are quietly switching seats behind her back.

To exchange seats, two players make eye contact and signal each other non-verbally (for example, with a nod or a blink). Their signal commits them to exchange seats, and they may not switch with anyone else. If the player in the middle sees them switching, she tries to take one of the seats that is temporarily vacant. If she is successful, the player left standing starts a new round.

★ Model and practice making eye contact and non-verbal signals. Make sure they understand that they must follow through and exchange seats with the person with whom they made eye contact. This rule makes it more challenging for players to switch seats secretly.

★ Discuss when might be a good time to answer *no* to the question *Is this seat taken?* For example, if a player has been in the middle for some time, it may be kind to give him a seat and allow a new player to take a turn in the middle.

★ Players can create guidelines for how to keep this game moving and avoid excluding anyone.

Material: Beach ball

One-team version

Players stand in a circle. A beach ball is hit aloft, and each player must hit the ball at least once before it falls to the ground. The ball may be hit only with hands, and may not be grabbed or held. Players may hit the ball more than once as long as they're helping keep it in play. Play continues until all have hit the ball.

Two-team version

Players form two teams. Teams stand on either side of a line. Keeping the ball aloft at all times, a team must hit the ball at least twice on their side before sending the ball to the other team. Possible goals: keeping the ball in play among the whole group for as many hits as possible; passing the ball from one team to another as many times as possible while keeping to the two-hits-per-side minimum; hitting the ball among teammates five times (or some other number) before returning it to the other team.

Variations

- Count hits. Keep the ball aloft for as many hits as possible before it falls. Set a goal (30, 50, 75, or 100 hits) to add incentive.
- Keep time. Set goals, such as all players hit the ball in less than one minute. The group can record its personal best, then try to better it another time.
- Draw a circle on the floor or ground, and say players may not step inside the line.

Also known as All Hit Moonball

Materials: Rubber chicken or other object to pass; category cards prepared in advance (cards may relate to curriculum or be general-information topics)

The point of this game is to not be left holding the chicken. Players sit in a circle. Select someone to be It, who holds the chicken. The leader says to It (for example), *Name five American presidents. Pass the chicken!* As soon as the leader says *Pass the chicken!* It passes the chicken to the right. It tries to follow the leader's direction (in this example, It tries to name five presidents) while the chicken continues around the circle. If the chicken makes it all the way around the circle and returns to It before It names five presidents, she remains It. If It succeeds in naming five presidents, the player holding the chicken when the response is completed (in this example, when It says the fifth president's name) becomes the new It.

Example categories

Nouns that begin with *m*; vegetables; musical groups; cereals; rivers in the United States; combinations of numbers that add up to 21.

✶Model and practice passing the chicken.

Variations

- Player who is It sits or stands in the middle of the circle and is given a task such as answering math problems or unscrambling words. The others begin passing the chicken. The object is to complete the task before the chicken gets back to the person who started passing it around the circle.

- Two players may stand in the middle and help each other complete the task.

- Tasks may be written on slips of paper; It draws the task out of a hat.

- It can name the category.

Also known as Name Six and Around the World

The goal is for the group to count up to a chosen number with only one person speaking at a time. The leader announces the number. Anyone can begin the count, and anyone can continue the count until the target number is reached. The counting comes from random players following no pattern or sequence, one person speaking a number at a time. A person may say only one number in a turn, but may have multiple turns. The challenge is to avoid having more than one person speak at a time. If more than one player says a number at the same time, the counting starts from the beginning again.

✶Model and practice counting without speaking at the same time. Do a trial round.

Variations

- Begin with a low target number and increase as the group gets more able to count without overlaps.

- Set up the rule that everyone must call out at least once (the target number must be greater than the number of people in the group).

- Count down from a target number, instead of up to it.

- Use names of players in the group instead of numbers. Try to say the name of every player in the group in random order until all have been named (without overlaps, of course).

- Time the counting (or naming) to try to improve the group's best time.

Also known as Count Up or Count Down

Radio

Players sit in a circle, with room for another circle surrounding them on the outside. Each syllable of the word *radio* has its own hand gesture: *ra* (pronounced *ray*) is one hand, palm down, on top of your head pointing left or right; *di* (pronounced *dee*) is one hand, palm down, under your chin pointing left or right; *o* is both hands pointing out to any player in the circle.

The game begins with somebody saying *ra* and making the gesture. If the beginning player points to the left, then the game is passed to the player on the left, who must then quickly say *di,* and pass the next move by pointing to the left or right. That player points with both hands, palms together, to someone in the circle (across from them) saying *o* while looking at the eyes of the person to whom she is pointing. That person starts another round with *ra.* If a player makes a mistake or takes too much time, she is out of the circle and becomes a heckler at the perimeter of the circle.

The hecklers whisper, hoping to confuse and distract the people who are still playing. Play until there are only two people left.

★Model and practice the three hand signals, appropriate heckler actions, and what response time is fast enough. Emphasize that the players who are out remain an active part of the game, by heckling. You may want to set a time limit.

Variation

- Use a three-syllable word other than radio, perhaps from the curriculum, or a phrase, such as *our class rocks!*

"RA"

"DI"

"O"

27

RADIO game

Materials: Note cards

The leader gives a note card to each player. Each player writes her name on the card, and answers two or three questions from the leader. The leader collects the cards and reads the answers aloud. Players have three guesses to identify the Rare Bird described on the card. The identified Rare Bird can then ask other players for questions and comments about what was learned.

Example Rare Bird questions

- List three things you like to do after school.
- List three of your favorite songs, foods, etc.
- List three characters you admire in _____ (a novel, drama, story, movie).
- What is your favorite piece of technology?
- What is something most people would not know about you?

Leaders can read several Rare Bird cards in one advisory and save others for future advisories.

✱Model and practice respecting players' differences. The purpose is to get acquainted and celebrate uniqueness. Review what constitutes an appropriate answer to a Rare Bird question.

Variation

- Connect questions to curriculum as a review for a test or at the end of the unit. Include a personal aspect to each curriculum-related question to connect it back to a responder. When guessing who the Rare Bird is, the class first verifies the accuracy of the answer, then guesses who the Rare Bird is based on the personal aspect of the answer.

  Example curriculum-related prompts: *List three elements on the Periodic Table and something you enjoy that can be made from one of them; write a simile and a metaphor for your favorite season*

  Also known as Who Am I?

Saggety Saggety, So Po Po

This game is an experience in cognitive dissonance! The leader says, *Saggety saggety, so po po* while repeating one accompanying motion, such as patting thighs, pointing to nose, or tapping knees. The leader says the chant again and this time does a new motion. When the leader starts the chant for the second time, the rest of the group joins in by saying the chant with the leader and doing the leader's **first** motion. When the leader says the chant for the third time and does a **third** motion, the group says the chant and does the leader's **second** motion. The activity continues in this way, with the chant getting faster and faster. The group is always one motion behind the leader.

Variation

- The leader says the chant twice, with two different accompanying motions, before the group joins in. In this variation, the group is two motions behind the leader.

Also known as Do What I Did

This game is great for practicing observational and memory skills. Partners face each other, turn around, change one thing about their appearance, and face each other again. The object is for each to detect what the other has changed. Played in partners, the game is low-risk. To increase the risk (and the fun), have two people stand in the middle of the circle and slowly turn around. The players in the circle look at the two people in the middle to memorize their appearance. The partners then go out of view, and each changes one thing about her appearance (or they change one thing about only one of them). They return to the circle and turn around slowly in the middle of the group. The other players get three guesses to name what was changed.

Variations

- Players can change more than one thing about their appearance.
- Shorten the amount of time players have to observe before the change is made to make the change harder to detect.
- Use observational skills on objects. The leader places a group of objects in the center of the circle and asks the players to memorize what's there. Players close their eyes, then the leader removes one thing, and players open their eyes and guess what's missing. You can also remove more than one object at a time.

Use Your Noodle

Material: Long swimming-pool noodle

Divide group into partners. With partners, players think of something they could act out while both hold a noodle (e.g., swing, telescope, rainbow, hula hoop, jump rope). Pairs take turns showing the group their creation, and the others guess what it is. The partners who guess correctly become the next pair to show their creation. The game continues until all players have used their noodle.

If the pair who guesses correctly has already had a turn, they pick who goes next.

✷ Model and practice choosing appropriate actions to show with the noodle. Discuss how to handle one pair necessarily being last, for example:

✷ Before starting, ask one pair to volunteer to be last.

✷ Tell the players that whoever is last today will be first the next time you play.

Variation

• Use a category, for example, characters or events from a known story or poem (Ahab looking through a telescope), vocabulary words from the curriculum (geometric shapes made with multiple noodles), or a tool (a noodle crosscut saw).

When the Cold Wind Blows

Materials: Circle of chairs

The number of chairs in the circle should be one less than the number of players. One player stands in the middle of the circle and says, *When the cold wind blows, it blows for anyone who*_____, filling in the blank with a category that applies to himself, such as *has a dog*. Everyone who fits that category, including the person in the middle, quickly finds a new place to sit. No player may return to the seat they left. The one player who doesn't find a seat stands in the middle of the circle and continues the game by saying, *When the cold wind blows, it blows for anyone who* _____, naming a new category that applies to himself. The activity continues for several rounds.

This lively activity is a great way for players to learn about each other and what they have in common with classmates. You can brainstorm a list of categories before beginning the activity.

✸ Model and practice safe movement across the circle and tapping a chair to claim it when more than one person is heading for it, to avoid crashing.

Variations

- To practice safe movement or review the process of the game, you can play with an equal number of chairs and players, so there is no scrambling for a seat.
- Establish categories such as interests, places, foods, or family.
- Limit categories to something that is not visible, which rules out focusing on clothing or appearance.

Also known as A Warm Wind Blows, A Hot Wind Blows, and The River Rises. Some versions of Fruit Basket Upset are similar.

Who What Where Am I?

Materials: Pre-made note cards naming people, places, and things related to a topic; tape or pins

The leader tapes a note card on the back of every player so that others know the identity, but the wearer of the note card does not. Players mingle and ask other players yes or no questions to determine who, what, or where they are. As more people guess who, what, or where they are, players who haven't yet guessed their identities can ask more open-ended questions.

Examples of topics and note cards

Topic: Weather
Note cards: Cumulus clouds, stratus clouds, dew point, hail, barometer, hurricane, etc.

Topic: Fractions
Note cards: 1/5, 50%, .20, ½, etc.
Extension: Players find another equivalent fraction after guessing their own.

✱Model and practice the mingling portion of the game to ensure appropriate social interaction, including greeting each other in a friendly way, noise level, movement, etc.

Variations

- Each player makes up one card to put on a partner.

- Players ask open-ended questions.

- Players have a mate related to the topic and try to find her or him. For example, if studying rocks, mates could be stalagmite and stalactite, lava and lava rock, gold and fool's gold (iron pyrite), etc.

Players stand in a circle, lower their heads, and close their eyes. The leader chooses a player to be the Winker by touching someone. Players raise their heads and open their eyes. To play, the Winker secretively makes eye contact with and winks at other players, one at a time, trying to avoid being seen by anyone but the target. When the Winker winks at a player, that player is "put to sleep" and slumps in his chair for the rest of the round. The rest of the players try to determine who the Winker is. When a player thinks he knows who the Winker is, he tells the leader. If he is wrong, he goes to sleep. If he is right, the round is over and a new round starts with a new Winker.

★ Model and practice that only the Winker winks. Demonstrate "going to sleep."

Variation

- When a player thinks he knows the identity of the Winker, he whispers it to the leader. If the guess is wrong, the guesser must go to sleep. If the guesser is right, he stays in the game. When three players have correctly guessed who the Winker is, a new round starts.

Yes, No, Black or Blue

Material: List of prepared questions

Create two to four teams by counting off. Each team forms a line with players facing the leader. The leader asks one question of each of the players at the front of each line. Players must answer immediately and may **not** use the words *yes, no, black,* or *blue* in their answers, or forms of those words, like *bluish.* If they are too slow or say one of the four forbidden words, they go to the end of their line. Players who answer successfully go on the leader's side of the room. The leader moves quickly from team to team, asking a question of the player at the front of each line. In order to play fast enough to confuse players, the leader should prepare a list of questions beforehand. As more and more players find ways to answer the questions without using the taboo words, they join teammates on the other side of the boundary line.

The group can decide to end the game at an arbitrary moment or when all players have successfully answered a question and crossed over to the leader's side of the room.

Example questions

Are you a teacher?
What color is the sky?
Will the Vikings win the Super Bowl?
Are you wearing shoes?
What color is a tomato?
Are you eating lunch today?
Do you have ten fingers?
A penguin is black and what other color?
Do you have teeth?
The United States flag is red, white, and what other color?
Do birds fly?
Is ketchup red?
Can you ride a bike?

What color is ebony?
Doves are what color?
Do you like golf?
Can you ski?
What color is white paper?
What color are Sponge Bob's square pants?
Is Patrick a starfish?
Is Charlie Brown really a great guy?
What is today's date?
Can you belly dance?
What color is a blue jay?
Do you have red pajamas?
What color is a blackboard?
Is your hair green?

★Model and practice how to answer questions immediately so players see the expected response time. Discuss alternative color, affirmative, and negative answers.

Variations

• As players become familiar with the game, words like "maybe" and "perhaps" can be added to the list of unacceptable answers.

• Introduce the game at preparation time for standardized tests as a playful way of showing that the first answer isn't necessarily the best, and that some questions are tricky.

This is a form of the Concentration game. Everyone in a circle numbers off. The players must remember their numbers. Number one starts by calling out another number—any number in the circle except her own. Whoever is called must then quickly call out another number—any number except his own. Each player must listen for his/her number so when it is called the player can quickly call out someone else's. If a player doesn't respond quickly when her number is called, she must move to the highest numbered seat in the circle, and everyone moves down a seat toward the vacated seat to make room at the "end." The object is to get into seat number one. After each seat shift, some players will have new numbers.

Example round

In a circle of 19 seats, number one calls out number ten, but number ten doesn't call out another number fast enough. Number ten then must go to seat number 19 and everyone from seat 19 to seat 11 moves up one number. The person who was number 11 becomes number ten, number 12 becomes number 11, and so on.

★ Model and practice chair-changing and renumbering by doing a few trial rounds. Also, decide as a group what "quickly" means in this game, so there is a clear standard for eliminating someone based on the speed of their response when called on.

Variations

- Everybody has a number, but in assigning numbers, you skip one number, for example, number ten. When players call out numbers as fast as they can, if they go too slowly or use the number ten, they lose their seat and move to the highest numbered seat in the circle.

- Each person chooses and shares an animal action or sound and must watch for their action to be shown. The players then show their action and show someone else's. As with calling numbers, if they don't respond quickly, they must move to the last spot in the circle.

Zumi Zumi

Groups of seven to ten players sit in circles. A player in each circle is selected to begin in the role of Zumi Zumi, who has the highest status during the game. The person to the left of Zumi Zumi has the next highest, and so on around the circle. The chant starts with everyone saying: *AAAAAAAAHHHHH-HHHH* while spiraling their hands upwards. Then the patting-clapping rhythm begins: pat laps twice; clap hands twice; pat laps twice; clap hands twice. This sequence is maintained throughout play, including during speaking, while the play moves to different people in the circle when their names are called. The one called on says his own name on the pats and the next person's name on the claps. Here's what happens:

1. Warm-up, repeat until rhythm is established:
   Pat pat/*Zumi Zumi*
   Clap clap/silence

2. Go around the circle once. Zumi Zumi starts the action:
   AAAAAAAAHHHHHHHHHH (with hand gesture)
   Zumi: Pat pat/*Zumi Zumi*
   Clap clap/*Jack Jack*
   Jack: Pat pat/*Jack Jack*
   Clap clap/*Maria Maria*
   Maria: Pat pat/*Maria Maria*
   Clap clap/*Sophie Sophie*
   And so on around the circle.

3. After making it successfully around the circle with no rhythmic glitches, Zumi Zumi continues play, this time saying *Zumi Zumi* and calling the name of any person in the circle. The person called must respond in rhythm, by saying her name twice on the pats and any other person's name on the claps. When a person delays or makes a mistake, he moves into the chair just to the right of Zumi Zumi (the

lowest-status chair). The object of the game is to have a person with a higher status make a mistake, so she moves to the lowest status chair and others move up. Ultimately, Zumi Zumi makes a mistake, so the person to Zumi's left becomes the new Zumi Zumi, and a new round begins.

Example calling names randomly

Zumi: Pat pat/*Zumi Zumi*
Clap clap/*Greta Greta* (Zumi Zumi calls on someone out of sequence in the circle)
Greta: Pat pat/*Greta Greta*
Clap clap/*Clara Clara* (Greta calls on someone out of sequence in the circle)
Clara: Pat pat/*Clara Clara*
Clap clap/*Zumi Zumi* (Clara calls on someone out of sequence in the circle)

If Zumi Zumi misses the beat or makes any mistake, he gives up his chair to the person on his left, the new Zumi Zumi; everyone shifts up one seat, and the deposed Zumi Zumi goes to the lowest status chair, the one to the right of the new Zumi Zumi.

Variation

- Increase the challenge by using numbers instead of names. Count off starting with the player to Zumi Zumi's right, who is number one, player to her right is two, and so on up to Zumi, who does not take a number. The larger the number, the higher the status. For example, in a group of 20, player number 19 is second only to Zumi Zumi. Players then say numbers instead of names, except for Zumi Zumi, who continues to use the name Zumi Zumi.

Example using numbers

Zumi: Pat pat/*Zumi Zumi*
Clap clap/*to the three* (Zumi calls on the person three spaces to his right)
Player Three: Pat pat/*to the three*
Clap clap/*to the ten* (player three calls on the person seven spaces to her right)
Player Ten: Pat pat/*to the ten*
Clap clap/*Zumi Zumi* (player ten calls on Zumi)

Greetings Introduction

Greetings are a friendly, fun way to recognize and name everyone in the group—a quick and effective way to show that everyone belongs. We set standards for the greetings and create intentional, inclusive, carefully designed moments to ensure that the day starts well for everyone. The greeting builds connections and serves as an antidote to whatever else may be pulling students away from one another.

The *Tried and True* greetings are of two types: 1) the basic greetings (perhaps with a special voice, gesture, or other detail) that quickly go from person to person around or across the circle, and 2) more active greetings that include some playful, get-acquainted movement. The basic greetings are good for practicing everyday greeting skills, and the more active greetings offer challenge and fun after the group has a foundation in greeting skills.

Every greeting includes eye contact, a friendly tone, and a pleasant expression. If there is physical contact, it is gentle and respectful. The greetings are audible, so the whole group can witness the welcoming of each of its members.

Community Level 1, Acquainted: For newly formed groups to practice greeting each other; highly structured to support learning and correctly pronouncing names; clear, simple formats for greeters to follow; usually do not include physical contact

Community Level 2, Familiar: For groups who already know each others' names and are ready for variations with more complexity; may include physical contact or an object that is passed or tossed during the greeting

Community Level 3, Comfortable: For groups who do well at Levels 1 and 2; more complex rules and more risk taking; may include physical contact

List of Greetings

Greetings Contents

In basic greetings, each person greets the person next to him or someone across the circle with *Hello, (Marie)* or *Good morning, (Jamal)*, and the person greeted responds in a like manner. That person then greets the next person, and the process is repeated until all are greeted. The essentials of a greeting (courtesy, friendliness, respect) must always be present. Some basic greetings work well by having an individual greet the whole group and the whole group greet back.

When the basic greeting is passed **across** the circle, the greeter who initiates the greeting looks at the person greeted and speaks the greeting. The greeted person responds in kind:

Good morning, Shavon.

Good morning, Toua.

Variations

- The greeter walks over to someone, greets her, then takes the greeted person's chair as that person leaves to greet someone else. To help greeters identify who has not yet been greeted, use a visual signal: after you have been greeted, fold hands in lap, drop arms to sides, cross legs, etc. until everyone has been greeted.

- Add a handshake to the verbal greeting. Use a standard handshake or invent variations.

＊Model and practice a safe and courteous handshake. If students are inventing handshakes for the group, be sure they are clearly demonstrated before using them.

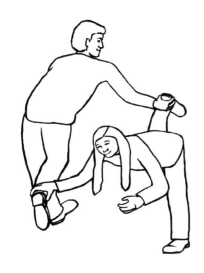

Ankle Shake Greeting   Community Level 2, Familiar

Two people face each other, raise their right feet, and shake each other's right ankle with their right hands while balancing and saying, *Good morning, Patrick! Good morning, Sonja!*

✱ Model and practice the gesture of raising feet and shaking ankles. Suggest raising right hands as if to shake hands, but lean forward and shake the right ankle instead.

Change Your Voice Greeting   Community Level 2, Familiar

Greet the group and then ask to be greeted back in a special voice or accent: *Good morning, everybody. I would like to be greeted in a* (sad voice, gleeful voice, British accent, Southern accent, etc.). Group responds in the voice the person chose: *Good morning, Jerome!*

Cow Greeting   Community Level 2, Familiar

Two people face each other. One person laces her fingers together with her thumbs pointing down. The other person pulls gently on her thumbs as if milking. The partners greet each other as they "milk."

Fishing Greeting

A person makes eye contact with someone else across the circle, casts an imaginary fishing line to that person, and reels him or her in. The other person walks toward the "fisher" as she is reeled in, and when she is near the fisher, she flops like a fish. The fish and the fisher greet each other, then the fish becomes the fisher, and the process is repeated with someone who hasn't yet been greeted. Use a body position or gesture (flop to one side, hang a hooked finger from a cheek, etc.) to signal having been greeted.

Fist Bump Greeting (Pound It!)

Greet each other with a gentle fist bump. Leader may choose to make this a silent greeting (eye contact is especially important) or use the Fist Bump Greeting as a quick simultaneous greeting when time is short.

✶Model and practice fist-bumping technique before beginning: make a fist, then gently tap partner's fist as *Good morning,*_____ is exchanged.

Floppy Fish Greeting

Two greeters extend their hands, touch wrists, and slap forearms lightly while simultaneously making floppy fish sounds. Decide ahead of time what sounds might be used.

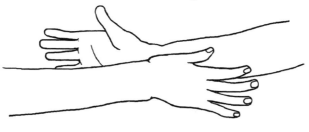

Formal Greeting

Greeters use titles and last names (*Good morning, Ms. Roberts. Good morning, Mr. Garcia.*), with or without a handshake.

Variation

Good morning, Sir James; Good morning, Lady Sharon; the greeter may bow or curtsy with faux formality.

Harley Greeting

One greeter creates motorcycle handlebars (fists together with thumbs pointing straight out to the sides); the other greeter grasps the thumb handlebars and makes a motorcycle revving sound while greeting.

High Five Greeting

Move in sequence around the circle, with a basic, easy-to-do gesture such as high five, double high five, high five/low five (greet with high five, respond with low five). Initially, everyone uses the same greeting (e.g., *Morning, _____*); later, let group members choose their own greetings and gestures to accompany their names.

Make Your Own Handshake Greeting

Greeters invent their own handshakes to accompany the greeting. The first person greets someone with her invented handshake, and the person greeted returns the same handshake. That person may pass on the same handshake or invent a new one as he greets the next person.

Microwave Greeting

Greet with a wave of the pinky finger.

Name with Gesture Greeting

A person greets the group adding a gesture to her name, like *Good morning, everyone. I'm Josie* (with a waving gesture). Group responds: *Good morning, Josie* (repeating the waving gesture).

Variations

- After all have greeted the group with a gesture, volunteers name and repeat the gestures of as many people as they can remember.
- Use the Cumulative Toss a Name variation of the Group Juggle game: *I am Kaitlin* (Kaitlin does her gesture), *and that is Ahmed* (do Ahmed's gesture). Ahmed repeats Kaitlin's, his own, and a third person's name and gesture, and tosses the ball to the third person. If someone can't remember a gesture, he can ask for help from the group and call on someone whose hand is raised to show him the gesture. The names and challenges accumulate as greeters try to recall all the names and gestures that came before.

Silent Greeting

Brainstorm ways to greet someone without using words. One at a time around the circle, greet each other silently using one of the modeled silent greetings.

✶ Model and practice possible silent greetings, such as nodding heads, smiling, making eye contact with raised eyebrows, shaking hands, winking, etc.

Variation

Look across the circle and make eye contact with at least three people. When everyone has been greeted, discuss what it felt like to be greeted silently, and the power of non-verbal communication.

Toothless Greeting

Before starting, greeters practice pulling their lips in to cover their teeth and talking and smiling with this "toothless" mouth. They then make a basic verbal greeting, but do it toothlessly. For variations, more elaborate verbal greetings can be delivered toothlessly.

Baseball Greeting

Baseball hits are singles, doubles, triples, or home runs. Greeters choose one of these four types of hits to determine whom they will greet. If a greeter calls a single, she greets the person next to her; if a double, she greets the person two chairs away; a triple is three chairs away; and a home run is four chairs away. Greeters may high-five people yet to be greeted as they pass by.

Everyone stands in a circle. The first "batter" announces the hit and moves to the appropriate person and greets him/her: *It's a double!* (Moves to the second person to his right) *Good morning, Ursula*. The greeted person repeats the process. Once a person has been greeted, he sits down. The greeting continues until everyone has been greeted, with the last batter greeting the first batter.

Variations

- Other sports metaphors can be used for this greeting. Use the appropriate scoring counts.

  Football: use points for touchdown, field goal, safety, five-yard gain, ten-yard gain, etc.

  Basketball: use free throw, two-point, and three-point baskets

Beach Ball Greeting

Material: Beach ball

Brainstorm favorite basic greetings (voice types, High Five, Microwave, Harley, etc). Write their names with a permanent marker here and there on a beach ball. One person starts by tossing the beach ball to another. The person who catches the ball chooses a greeting type that one of his hands is touching. Using that greeting, he greets the person who tossed him the ball, who replies with the same greeting. The person holding the ball tosses it to someone else, and the cycle continues until all have been greeted. As with all greetings across the circle, use a visual sign that a person has been greeted (fold hands in lap, drop arms to sides, etc.).

✸Model and practice being ready to catch the ball and tossing the ball appropriately. Make sure everyone understands that there is no signal to the recipient before the ball is tossed and there is no penalty for not catching the ball.

ACTIVE GREETINGS

Beanbag Toss Greeting

Material: Beanbag or other small, lightweight ball

One person starts by greeting someone verbally, making eye contact, and then tossing the beanbag to that person: *Good morning, Aiden* (pause until eye contact is made, then throw the beanbag to that person). The person receiving the beanbag greets the thrower and then continues by greeting another person and tossing the beanbag to her. The greeters must remember to whom they tossed the bag and from whom they received it. After people receive and toss the beanbag, they put their hands behind their backs to signal they have been greeted, which helps others see who has not. After everyone has been greeted, the first round is complete. In the second round, the challenge is to pass the beanbag duplicating the pattern of the first round.

✱Model and practice tossing the beanbag safely before playing the game. Participants must say the greeting and make eye contact before **softly** tossing the beanbag underhand. The objective is to go quickly and not pause to search for someone to greet, so attentiveness is essential. One way to encourage carefulness is to time the round, because tossing before getting eye contact is likely to cost time as players retrieve the ball and start again.

Variations

- For greater challenge (and fun), add beanbags and have several going simultaneously, all in the same route pattern.
- See Group Juggle and its variations on page 20 for activity versions of this greeting.

Elevator Greeting

Stand close together facing the same direction, as if in an elevator. Everyone keeps their eyes fixed on the space above the imaginary elevator door, where the floor indicator lights might be in an elevator. Each person greets and is greeted by two or three of the people closest to him or her (*Good morning, _____*). Challenge greeters to make the greeting friendly even though they are not looking at one another. Discuss the value of eye contact and whether it is possible to make up for the lack of eye contact with facial and other body gestures.

One-minute Mingle Greeting

Group members move to the center of the circle and greet as many people as they can in one minute. Remind students to follow the criteria for greetings (eye contact, saying the person's name, friendly voice, etc.—see page 41). The One-minute Mingle Greeting is great for groups with reliable greeting skills and when you have only a short time for greetings.

✴Model friendly greeting and any variations you choose.

Variations

- Group chooses a gesture and/or verbal variation for the greeting such as High Five Greeting with *How's it going, _____?* or Floppy Fish Greeting with *Good day, _____?*
- Group greets one another in as many different languages as they can.

Snake Greeting

The leader stands up, greets a neighbor, gets greeted in return, and moves on to greet the next person. As the leader moves on, the person she greeted stands and follows her, greeting the people the leader just greeted. The next person also becomes a greeter, and so on—a growing "snake" of people forms behind the leader. Once the leader has greeted everyone, she returns to her seat, and others follow in succession to their seats, until everyone is seated again.

Shares Introduction: Learning the Art of Conversation

In a healthy community, people come to know each other by talking, day by day, about themselves and their world. The following structures create a safe, encouraging environment for everyone in the classroom or advisory to share themselves and come to know and care about one another, with everyone included.

SHARE STRUCTURE	COMMUNITY LEVEL	CAN BE QUICK	PAGE
Individual Share	2		54
Interview Share	1		55
Partner Share	1	X	56
Table-top Share	1		58
Whip Share	1	X	59
Favorite Share Topics	1-3	X	60

Individual Share

This share format helps participants learn how to carry on meaningful conversations within a group—the kind of conversations that build relationships and social skills.

A student starts an interactive conversation with the group by making a brief statement or two about a topic (either assigned by the leader or chosen by the sharer). For example, *I'm going to spend next weekend at my cousin's house. It's his birthday on Saturday. I'm open for questions or comments.*

The group then asks questions or comments about the topic, directing each question or comment to the sharer. The quality of the sharing conversation depends on the audience's interesting, open-ended questions. The sharer fleshes out the story by answering questions and responding to comments.

✶Model and practice the format before inviting the group to volunteer to share. Pay particular attention to the quality of the questions, perhaps brainstorming some interesting, open-ended ones that call for more than single word answers. For example, *Was it fun?* could be replaced by *What was the most fun thing about it?*

Variations

- **Longer Talks:** Participants can lengthen the brief statement made by the sharer. The sharer can give a one- or two-minute talk on the topic. Eventually, participants may learn to speak at length to a group on a topic very familiar to them.

- **News Flash** or **Burning Share**: A student tells the headline of something new (News Flash) or something he just can't wait to tell (Burning Share). The leader may ask the class, *Who has a news flash?* or, *Does anyone have a burning share?* The Individual Share structure is followed to learn more about the news or burning topic.

Also known as Interactive Share or the Standard Share

This share format helps participants break the ice and begin to develop skills for an interactive conversation by providing a structure for it.

The leader (sometimes with input from others) identifies an interview theme or topic and the group brainstorms questions to ask about it. A scribe writes the questions on a chart. Participants form partners (methods for forming partners are described under Partner Share) and interview each other, taking turns asking and answering the questions. The goal is to elicit three pieces of information about each person on the identified topic.

✶ Model and practice forming good, open-ended questions.

Variations

- **Share Out:** A few participants report out the three pieces of information they **heard** from their partner (not their own information).

- Reflect after the interview on which questions drew the most interesting information. This will help participants learn how to ask interesting questions.

- **Press Conference:** After interview questions have been generated, the whole group interviews one person on a chosen topic (a topic especially suitable for that particular interviewee). Questions may be asked round-robin, by raising hands, or by drawing name sticks.

Partner Shares often feel safer than Individual Shares, because of the more private, one-to-one context for the conversation.

The leader names a topic and specifies a length of time to share. In pairs, partners take turns sharing about the topic. The leader may announce a time warning halfway through when the pairs should switch so partners share equally.

Partner Share can be livened up by various methods for forming partners. Possibilities include:

- **High Five Partner Share:** Participants turn to a right- or left-hand neighbor and form a partnership with a "high five." The partners proceed to discuss the topic.

- **Clock Partners:** Pre-establish partners for every hour or for the four quarter-hours. The leader announces, *Meet with your one o'clock partner,* or *Meet with your half-past the hour partner.* Write the names on a drawing of a clock for reference.

- **Seasonal Partners**: Pre-establish partners for summer, fall, winter, and spring. Write the names down for reference.

- **Compass Partners**: Pre-establish partners for the directions on a compass. Younger participants may be limited to north, south, east, and west, while older participants can also use northeast, southeast, southwest, and northwest. Write partnerships down for reference.

- **Yes:** Participants look around the circle until they make eye contact with someone. At the instant eye contact occurs, one or both say *Yes!* and the two become partners.

★ Before the first Partner Share, the leader models with a student, and the group practices an appropriate share. Modeling should demonstrate good listening and asking socially inclusive questions such as *What's your opinion?*

Variations

- **Share Out:** Partner Share is followed by reporting to the whole group something that was heard during the share. Instruct each person to share out for their partner. Limit the share-out to one thing, or a highlight. The leader may tell the number of share-outs that will be heard and then select that number of people to share, or take that number of volunteers.

- **Inside-outside Circles:** Participants number off by ones and twos. All the **ones** form an inner circle facing out, and all the **twos** form an outer circle facing in. Everyone in the inner circle faces a partner in the outer circle. Partners share (usually 30 seconds each). After one minute, the leader calls time and instructs the circles to move one position to the right or left. The circles move and new partners form. Share again on a new question or the same question. The leader decides how many rounds and how much time per Inside-outside Partner Share.

Table-top is a lively, playful structure in which participants have conversations within changing groups. Each conversation is structured with a specific topic or question.

Participants begin by mingling politely among the whole group. The leader calls out the size of the table group (for example, *Table for three!*) and participants arrange themselves into groups of the number called and stand still. If tables are available, they may actually sit at tables, but imaginary tables work, too. Participants may not exclude anyone from their group nor go out of their way to create a group consisting of friends. Once table groups are formed, the leader announces a topic to be discussed and the amount of time for discussion. For example, *Table for five*. (Pause for tables to form.) *Two minutes on the importance of caring for a pet.* Groups discuss. The leader watches the time and gives a signal for quiet when the time runs out.

The leader can help guide conversations by quickly appointing a group facilitator for each Table-top Share, or the group can designate one person.

✴Model and practice making sure everyone is part of a table group. If the group doesn't divide exactly into the number called, participants need to invite any extras to their tables. Begin the sharing for each round only when everyone has a seat at a table.

Variation

- Play multiple rounds. The leader can announce the same or a new, larger number for the next table tops. For example, start with tables for three, then tables for four, then five. To encourage mingling and getting acquainted with everyone, aim for variety in the mix of people in table groups. Shares must become briefer as table sizes become larger.

Whip sharing strengthens inclusivity because everyone gets a chance to contribute, and the risk is kept low by the shortness of each response.

The leader provides a question or a sentence stem *(What are your favorite weekend activities?* or *On weekends, my family likes to ____)* and every participant around the circle responds with a word or phrase or brief statement that completes the sentence.

✳ Model and practice giving participants time to think of their responses before starting the whip share. Ask for a thumbs-up to indicate readiness, and start when most have an answer. At the beginning, allow participants the option of passing if they are not comfortable speaking in front of classmates, but as comfort builds, everyone should be expected to contribute something.

Variations

- **Option to Pass:** At the end of the Whip Share, the leader may come back to those who passed in order to include everyone.

- **Who Remembers?** When the Whip Share is complete, extend the participants' familiarity with one another by asking them to recall information, or synthesize what the group has shared. For example, *Who remembers who wanted to be a doctor? Who loved chocolate ice cream? Who went camping this weekend? What was the most common weekend activity? What was the most (or least) popular movie?*

Also known as Round-robin or Go-round Share

Favorite Share Topics

Most topics lend themselves to a variety of share structures. The topic must be narrower and more specific for fast shares such as Whip Share or Table-top Share with larger numbers at the table. The same topic or question can be expanded for Partner Shares or small numbers of people in a Table-top Share. Interview Shares and Individual Shares work best initially with a broader question to explore.

NARROW, SPECIFIC SHARE TOPIC OR QUESTION	BROADER, DEEPER SHARE TOPIC OR QUESTION
As a little kid, my hero was___.	As little kid, my hero was___because he/she___.
Someone who has been significant in my life	Someone who has been significant in my life and what they did or do for me
What's the most important thing a person should know about you?	What's the most important thing a person should know about you? Why?
What is your favorite spirit day/hat day/wacky-tacky day?	What do you like about your favorite spirit day/hat day/wacky-tacky day?
My career choice at this time is___.	My career choice at this time is___and___is my inspiration for choosing it.
If I could change one thing about school, it would be___.	If I could change one thing about school, it would be___ and that would improve things by___.
Who else in your family has your first or middle name?	What is the story behind your first or middle name?
Name someone you admire.	Name someone you admire, and tell why you admire him/her.
What is something you learned when you were younger?	How has something you learned when you were younger helped you or others?

NARROW, SPECIFIC SHARE TOPIC OR QUESTION	BROADER, DEEPER SHARE TOPIC OR QUESTION
If you could relive any age, what age would it be?	If you could relive any age, which age would it be, and why?
One of my goals this year is____.	How will achieving your goal this year make your life better?
Our family likes to____.	What does your family like to do, and when, how, or where do they do it?
Last weekend I____(activity or event).	Tell about your activity or event last weekend and include who, what, where, and when.
If topics: If I could change one thing about the world, it would be____. If I could get a tattoo, it would be____. If I could go anywhere in the world I would go to____.	Pose an *if* question and ask for an explanation of why.
What is your favorite____? family ritual season food	What is your favorite____and why? What's best about it? Tell us more about it.
What is one thing you do to stay healthy?	What is challenging about something you do to stay healthy, and how do you stick with it?
Name one thing that stresses you in life.	Name one thing that stresses you in life, and tell how you handle it.
What was the best gift you ever gave to someone?	Tell about the best gift you ever gave to someone. What was it? To whom did you give it? Why was it great?
Name an injury or illness you have had.	Tell about what happened when you were injured or ill.
Name someone you know who has acted bravely.	Share about a time when you were brave.
Name one quality of friendship that you value.	What are the qualities of a really good friend?
Name an adult you admire and one quality they possess.	Describe the kind of person you would like to be when you are an adult.
(No narrow topic; this topic best explored deeply)	If you had $200 and had to give $100 away to someone, whom would you give it to, and why?

FAVORITE SHARE TOPICS

Acknowledgments and Cheers Introduction

One important way that people support each other in a community is through kind words: words that give credit where it is due, words that compliment us for our kindnesses and our skills. The best acknowledgments are specific descriptions of what was said or done well (not comments about how a person looks or general compliments). Specific compliments encourage us to continue doing positive things. When we experience a public acknowledgment, we feel more connected and valued, and we rise to be our best selves.

We can conclude or celebrate a quality moment with a cheer. One of the best ways to build a strong, supportive community is to make a habit of speaking up for each other with acknowledgments and cheers. Included here are three tried and true structures for acknowledgments, and a variety of cheers that can be done quickly to bolster spirits.

ACKNOWLEDGMENTS AND CHEERS	COMMUNITY LEVEL	PAGE
Acknowledgment Buffet	2	64
Secret Friend	3	65
Tap Someone Who	2	66
CHEERS		
The Alligator	1	68
The Beatnik	1	68
The Clam	1	68
Fireworks	1	68
High Five	1	68
Invent Your Own	1	68
Noiseless Cheer	1	69
Round of Applause	1	69
Two Snaps Up	1	69

Acknowledgment Buffet

Give each person a paper plate and have him write his name in the middle of the plate. He will then exchange his plate with another person. Each person will write an acknowledgment of the other person on that person's plate. The group members exchange plates with others and write acknowledgments as much as time permits. After the final exchange, the leader asks people to return the plates to their owners (the name in the middle of the plate). Give the group time to read and reflect on what has been written.

✱ Model and practice what constitutes an appropriate acknowledgment before exchanging plates.

Variation

- **Pat on the Back:** People trace their hands on the paper plates and tape them to their backs. They circulate randomly, using an inside-outside circle (see page 57), or another way the leader instructs, and ask others to write acknowledgments on their paper plates. When the leader calls time, everyone removes his or her plate and reads the acknowledgments.

The leader makes name cards for everyone in the group. At the beginning of the day or week, people randomly draw a name card and keep it secret. The name drawn becomes the person's secret friend for the day or week. Each person pays attention to what her secret friend does and says, so that by the end of the day or week, each can share a specific descriptive acknowledgment of the secret friend.

Secret Friend acknowledgments can be shared in pairs or as a share-out in front of the whole group.

✷Model and practice identifying positive actions and characteristics to be acknowledged, such as behavior that shows social skills (such as the cooperation, communication, assertion, responsibility, engagement, empathy, and self-control)) or are consistent with the group's rules.

✷When doing Secret Friend over a week, the leader should remind the group each day to continue to observe during the week. The daily reminders are helpful, especially the first time this is done across a week's time.

Variation

- **Greeting Card**: Write the acknowledgment(s) as a greeting card or letter. The leader may provide a story starter, such as *This week I have seen you___*. The observer/acknowledger may decorate the card with images related to the positive feedback.

Tap Someone Who

Group members sit in a circle. The leader asks all members to close their eyes. The leader chooses about four volunteers to be tappers. Tappers stand outside the circle. Remaining people continue to keep their eyes closed. In a calm voice everyone can hear, the leader tells the tappers to *Tap someone who* and names a category from a list (see below, or of the leader's invention). Tappers move quietly around the room gently tapping the shoulders of people they feel fit each category.

The leader gives ample time for tapping before announcing a new category. Play should continue for several categories. The leader may select new tappers at any point.

Example categories

Tap someone who . . .

is a good listener.
will invent something.
you would like to be stranded on a desert island with.
is as good as___ (gold, a chocolate sundae, etc.).
would keep a secret if you asked him or her to.
is a good friend.
you don't often work with, but would like to get to know better.
helped you today.
would make a good (leader, accountant, computer repair specialist, dancer, comedian, etc.).
makes you laugh.
you'd like to have lunch with.
you admire.
you would go with on a trip to Fargo, North Dakota; New York City; Hawaii; etc.
has taught you something.
you'd invite to join your rock 'n' roll band—singers, roadies, guitar players, bus drivers, etc.

★ Model and practice gently tapping people on the shoulder.

Variation

After the tapping is over and eyes are open, reflect with the group:
How did it feel to be tapped? Why?
How did it feel to be the tapper? Why?
Do you have other ideas for questions we can ask?
How does this activity help us to make a more caring classroom?
Do you have any ideas how to make this acknowledgment more fun or meaningful?

The Alligator

Stretch both arms straight out in front as if to make alligator jaws; at the signal, do one big clap.

The Beatnik

Snap fingers in unison.

The Clam

Interlock fingers; at the count, clap palms of hands together.

Fireworks

Place palms together in a gesture of prayer, move them upward as if fireworks being launched. Open hands outward and away from each other, fingers dancing and jiggling as a burst of fireworks, and let them float downward. Make sounds to accompany the fireworks: blasting *(krsh!)* as hands move upward, exploding *(paah!)* as the fireworks burst into color in the sky, and raining down *(shhshhshhshhshh)* as the sparkles settle to earth. Add an acknowledged person's name at a chosen point (blastoff, explosion, sparkling down).

High Five

Do high five around the circle, in partners, etc.

Invent Your Own

The best cheers will be the ones the students create. Have them design cheers that relate to the purpose of the acknowledgment. For example, to acknowledge somebody for helping her on the phone with homework, the student could mime picking up a phone, dialing, and then say, *Thank you, homework help line!*

Noiseless Cheer

Hearing-impaired people use this gesture to acknowledge others. Open hands, palms out, are raised to ear level and wiggled.

Round of Applause

Clap while moving your hands in a circle parallel to your body (vertical plane).

Two Snaps Up

As a group, start with hands waist high. At the count, raise hands to shoulder height and snap once, then lower hands back to waist level. Raise hands again to shoulder height and snap again.